Translator's Preface.

The three following Essays, although written some time back, appear to bear so strongly on a question daily and hourly discussed among ourselves, that I make but one apology for presenting them in an English form, which is to the illustrious author, whose sentiments (notwithstanding all the attention I have given to the task) I cannot but fear I may yet have failed in representing.

The Translation contained in the following pages originated in the simple desire to facilitate the access to sentiments deemed beneficial.

He who undertook this pleasing and benevolent task, has been removed from this earthly scene. Let it be hoped that this solemn truth may add interest to his labours for others, and that his earnest wishes for their benefit may be in some measure realized.

Preface.

When I collected these moral sketches, which were written at different times and under varying circumstances, I did not think that I needed to add anything to them. A recent event, however, has determined me, in now publishing them, to say a few words more.

Having been called upon on the 30th of last April to take the chair at a meeting of the Protestant Bible Society, I expressed myself in these terms:—

> What is after all, speaking religiously, the great question, the most important question which at present occupies the minds of men? It is the question in debate between those who acknowledge and those who deny a supernatural, certain, and sovereign order of things, although inscrutable to human reason. The question in dispute, to call things by their right names, between supernaturalism and naturalism. On the one side, unbelievers, pantheists, pure rationalists, and sceptics of all kinds. On the other, Christians.
>
> "Amongst the first, the best still allow to the statue of the Deity, if I may make use of such an expression, a place in the world and in the human soul; but to the statue only,—an image, a marble. God himself is no longer there. Christians alone possess the living God.
>
> "It is the living God whom we need! Our present and future safety requires that faith in supernatural order, that respect for and submission to supernatural order should again pervade the world and the human soul,—the greatest minds as well as the simplest, the most elevated classes as well as the most humble. The truly efficacious and regenerating influence of religious belief depends on this condition. Without it, all is superficial, almost worthless.

"We may, at this day, with safety strive to re-animate and propagate the Christian faith; for liberty—religious and civil liberty—is abroad to prevent faith begetting tyranny and oppression of the conscience—another sort of impiety. The friends of liberty of conscience may fearlessly return to the God of the Christian; there are no longer, nor will there ever henceforth be, captives or slaves around his altars. Let, then, Christian faith and piety return; they will bring back in their train neither injustice nor violence. Doubtless, much care must be taken and many contests sustained, in order that religious liberty may be preserved unharmed in the midst of growing religious fervour; but this beautiful harmony will be attained, and will do honour to our time. Between Christians of different communions there may exist henceforth but those struggles of free faith and piety, which alone are permitted by the law of God, and are alone worthy of His attention."

These words have been remarked upon, and either approved of or objected to, in very different senses, by philosophers and by Christians.

On the day after they had been uttered, Mr. Louis Veuillot said in *l'Univers*,—"Monsieur Guizot made a speech which we have read with a sentiment of respect and sympathy, mingled with some grief. It would be impossible for us to do otherwise than highly honour the man who makes, even *a-propos* of a movement which we do not approve and which is far from being good, so noble a profession of Christian faith. It would be impossible for us not to regret deeply that so great and generous a spirit, one so well formed to comprehend unity, and so naturally disposed to submit himself to it, not only does not perceive that he is out of place amidst the separated members of the mother church, but even takes the lead in a movement which has been and still is opposed strongly to the doctrine of that church. What is Christianity? It is authority. What is Protestantism? It is free inquiry; and the Protestant Bible Society is the practice of free inquiry driven to its last and indefinite limit."

On the same day M. Charles Gourand said in *l'Ordre*— "Monsieur Guizot's speech breathes at once the spirit of faith in revelation and love of religious liberty. But he must conform his practice to his precepts. If it is thought that there exists no serious difference between a rationalist, however thoroughly convinced and honest he may be, whether called Plato, Descartes, or Leibnitz, and an atheist; if it is thought that apart from the teaching of the church all religious belief is superficial and nearly vain; then there is no room for hesitation, it is within the pale of the true church, of that great Catholic Church, which from St. Paul to De Maistre, has bent under the same discipline so many haughty spirits and great minds, that an asylum and pardon are to be sought. For if it be allowable to insinuate that atheism is logical rationalism, it is still more so to say that Protestantism is but inconsistent rationalism. In fact, either private judgment has the sway in matters of faith; and has it entirely, for who can flatter himself that he can take a part in free enquiry and say to it, 'Thus far shalt thou go, and no further!' or else it is authority which bears rule. But neither can she, any more than private judgment, do so by halves; she must have all or nothing. A compromise between the two systems is chimerical; *fusion* is still more hopeless, if possible, in religious than in political systems."

I shall not discuss the matter; I shall lay aside every personal question, every controverted point, every argument. Controversy opens the abyss which it pretends to fill, for it adds the obstinacy of self-love to differences of opinion. To overcome objections raised by honourable and sincere men gives me but little pleasure. I have a higher desire. I aspire to unite myself with them in the truth. Two ideas fill my mind, and predominate on this subject. I wish to set them forth in pure and bright light. If I succeed, if I can transfuse them into other minds, they will do their own work, and render unnecessary the controversy from which I abstain.

It would not be worth while to live if we gathered from a long life, no other fruit than a little experience and prudence in the affairs of this world, against the moment of leaving it. The prospect of human affairs, and the inward trials of the soul, afford brighter gleams, which spread themselves over the mysteries of nature and the destiny of man, and of this universe in the midst of which man is placed. I have received from practical life, deeper insight into these formidable questions, than meditation and science have ever given me.

The first and most important is this. The world and mankind do not explain themselves naturally and simply by themselves, by the sole virtue of the fixed laws which preside over them, or of the passing determinations which display themselves. Neither nature and her power, nor man and his acts, suffice to explain the prospect which human intellect contemplates or catches a glimpse of.

Then, as nature and man are insufficient to explain themselves, it follows that they are equally so to govern themselves. The government of the universe and of the human race differs from that aggregate of natural laws and facts which human reason observes there, as much as from the accidental laws and facts which human liberty introduces.

That is to say, that beyond the natural and human order which falls under our notice, is the supernatural and superhuman order which God directs and develops beyond the reach of our researches.

And when man ceases to believe this to be the case, ceases to believe in this supernatural order, and to live under the influence of this belief, then disorder intrudes among men and societies of men, and there commits ravages which would infallibly lead to their destruction, did not the wise goodness of God restrain them in their faults, and render them incapable of absolutely withdrawing themselves from the empire of truth, much as they may misunderstand it.

That the religious question is now fairly raised between those who, more or less explicitly and from a variety of motives, do not admit this supernatural order of things, that is, the greater number of philosophers whatever their denomination; and those who really admit it, that is, all Christians; is what no serious mind can deny.

Do I mean then to put on a level and confound all who disallow supernatural order, whether unbelievers or sceptics, atheists or rationalists?

God forbid I should imagine, far less express, anything so absurdly and heinously wicked! I know the happy inconsistencies of the mind of man, and the clouds which, to the eyes of the most learned, cover the paths they are treading. Surely, between the impious man who denies God, and the rationalist who is satisfied that, without going further than nature leads, and taking for granted I know not what transformation, he has found and established a God,—the interval is immense; immense, doubtless, in the eye of divine justice, as well as of human equity. And such is our levity and intellectual depravity, that in this vast space eminent minds and ingenuous hearts may, and, alas! probably always will be met, at every step between gross materialism and pure deism. The variety and forms of error are infinite and infinitely varied; and man, when falling into it, makes infinite efforts to retain some fragments of truth; and God permits him to succeed or honestly persuade himself he has done so, which will one day prove his excuse or else be to him a plank of safety.

I admit all distinctions, all inequalities, all sincerity. I only affirm two things; one, that all the philosophic schools of our day, different as may be their systems and merits, have this in common, that they deny this supernatural order, and strive to explain and govern man and the world without its aid; the other, that where faith in this order does not exist, the bases of moral and social order are deeply and increasingly shaken, man having ceased to live in presence of the only power which really surpasses him, and which is able at once to satisfy and direct him.

Natural order is the field open to man's knowledge. Supernatural order is so in degree to his faith and hope; but knowledge does not penetrate it. In the order of nature man exercises a share of action and power; in supernatural order he has but to submit. It has been said in the spirit of conciliation and peace, "Religion and Philosophy are sisters who should mutually respect and protect each other." The words bear the stamp of the chimæras of human pride. Philosophy springs from man; it is the work of his mind. Religion comes from God; man receives it, and often alters it after reception, but he does not create it. Religion and philosophy are not sisters. They are daughters, the one of "Our Father which is in Heaven," the other of mere human genius. And their condition in this world is no more equal than their origin. Authority is the apanage of religion; liberty is that of philosophy.

I now approach the second of the dominant ideas, more than ever essential to true order, and which I wish to bring prominently forward.

"Christianity," says M. Veuillot, "is authority." It is true; Christianity is authority, but it is not authority only; it is the entire man, all his nature and all his destiny. Now, moral obedience is the nature and destiny of man; that is, obedience in a state of liberty. God created man to obey His laws; he created him free that he might morally obey. Liberty, like authority, is of divine institution; the work of man is revolt and tyranny.

In the social state, authority and liberty need protection, and both have a right to it. There is need of control, both for the governors and the governed, for both are men. Hence political laws and institutions which now sustain, now limit power; that is, which decide on what conditions and by what means authority is to be exercised and liberty secured.

What is the measure of authority necessary for Government, what the extent of liberty possible in human society? What are the means of action, what the pledges to be given alike to authority and religion? Matters depending on circumstances, variable according to the times, the social condition, the manners, races, and different degrees of civilization amongst nations. It belongs to the politician to solve these questions.

When Christianity appeared in the world, appeal was first made to liberty, the moral liberty of man. This was necessary, as it came to abolish ancient creeds which were protected by the established powers. In this struggle, not only did growing Christianity never attack or question the existing authorities, but it formally acknowledged their rights, and while respecting them herself ordered others to respect them also. But at the same time, as regards the relations of men towards God, she appealed to the free consciences of men, and affirmed in principle the same liberty which she practised. "We must obey God rather than man," said St. Peter. "Try the spirits whether they be of God," said St. John. "I speak as to wise men, judge ye what I say," said St. Paul.

At the creation God prescribed obedience to men under penalty of death; in the day of regeneration God set man's liberty in motion to begin the work of salvation.

There is no partiality with God, no void in his designs; when he acts upon man he takes human nature as a whole; our inclinations, our wants, our interests, our various rights are all before his eyes. He at the same time provides for and satisfies all; authority as well as liberty, liberty as well as authority. It is a dangerous mistake to misapprehend this complete and harmonious character of the divine work, and to mutilate it by seeking weapons in it for our human dissensions. Christ came to save mankind, not to give a party triumph. Christianity began by invoking liberty and giving her action. She then overcame, and set forth her authority. She then accommodated herself to the various forms and degrees of authority and liberty which the course of events brought out here and there in the world. Associated with the destinies and deeds of the human race, Christianity has suffered for our mistakes and faults, and has been often altered and compromised by the waywardness of human liberty and authority. But by her origin and essence she is beyond the reach of their struggles, inexhaustible in her virtue to heal contradictory evils, and always ready to afford help on the side where danger threatens or redress is needed.

In the actual state of society and disposition, it is authority, and with authority order, which are in danger: Christianity owes them all her support. I know of no greater falsehood or more gross perversion than that of the men who in this day strive to turn the Christian religion to the promotion of that brutal and foolish anarchy which they denominate social democracy. The gospel and history are equally repugnant to this absurd profanation. The cause of civil authority and of the Christian religion is clearly common. Divine order and human order, the State and the Church, have common dangers and common enemies. May God grant them common wisdom; for while at the same time each separately and both in concert must re-establish authority in her position and rights, they must also solve another and newer problem, and satisfy other and pressing wants.

I have nothing to say to those men who think that for many ages society in Europe, and especially in France, governments as well as the minds of men, have pursued a totally wrong road, and that there is nothing in the prevailing character and tendency of our actual civilisation but error, corruption and decay. I understand that, thinking thus, they deem retrograde reaction necessary as well as legitimate, and venture upon it accordingly. As regards such, I can but express my profound conviction;

that they will have no success. Even were they right, they would have no success. If they were right, modern society would be condemned to perish; we should make progress in decay; but we should not return to what is past. But they are not right. No one is more convinced than I am of the immense mistakes and fatal errors of our day. No one more fears and abhors the influence which the revolutionary spirit exercises among us, and the danger with which that threatens us; a human Satan, at once sceptical and fanatical, anarchical and tyrannical, eager to deny and to destroy, incapable alike of creating aught that can live or of allowing aught to be created and exist under its eye. I am one of those who think it absolutely necessary to overcome this fatal spirit, and to replace in honor and power the spirit of order and faith, which is the spirit of life and safety. But I do not believe that this revolutionary spirit preponderates in modern minds. I do not believe that our civilization has been for ages mere mistake and corruption. I do not believe in the irremediable evil, or inevitable decay of my time and of my country.

The characteristic, the most important part of modern civilisation is the prodigious increase of the ambition and power of man. Recall what has taken place in past ages and that which now goes on, the long series and vast mass of human toil and success of all kinds in all places, the many secrets laid bare by science, the many monuments raised by genius, the riches created by industry, the progress of justice, the ease introduced into the condition of the lowly as well as the great, the weak as well as the strong; man marching as a master over the whole space of the earth which he inhabits, and gauging with an accurate eye the worlds which he cannot reach; the mind spreading her discoveries and ideas through every recess of human society; matter in its every form subjected and made subservient to man's use; this expansive and ascendant ardour which circulates in the whole social body; this activity universal, incessant, and unceasingly fruitful, which puts every thing in motion, and works for the general good. Never has man advanced so rapidly to the conquest and dominion of the world; never in his capacity and with the powers of man has he exercised such a rule over nature and society.

I know how much there is here of evil and danger, of intoxication and miscalculation; these, however, are not the symptoms of decline, they are those of greatness and futurity. It is with this great fact, this enormous increase of the power and ambition of humanity, that Church and State, Christian and civil government have to deal henceforth. When, with the help of God and outward circumstances, they shall have brought man back to respect those eternal laws which he has so foolishly misconstrued; when they shall have again placed bounds to his power, and subdued the vanity of his pride, man will still remain powerful and haughty, conscious of his strength and full of desire for the rights which have excited his ambition. Where there is strength, by natural harmony and in a certain measure, power and liberty follow. What hereafter will be that measure? What share of influence will man, each individual man, exercise on his own and the public destiny? That is the problem; it may be solved, it cannot be eluded. The spirit of liberty has entered society in the train of the labours and progress of humanity; it may be kept in its proper sphere, it cannot be expelled.

Everywhere civil governments are aware of this, and act accordingly. I see the deepest injustice prevailing towards the governments of our day. It is false that they are indifferent to the welfare and progress of nations. It is false that they only look to stability and tyranny. They may doubtless feel personal passions, old errors; but whatever their form, they are all, from motives of prudence or duty, seriously impressed with the necessity of respecting the rights and ameliorating the condition of men. And those most opposed to liberal appearances make every day, in their laws and practice, a multitude of changes favourable to justice and liberty.

I say, too, that European governments, amidst the storms of the last sixty years, have conducted themselves, taking all into account, with great moderation. Their dignity incessantly insulted, their existence attacked, they have not given way, either during the struggle or after the victory, to those excesses of passion or power with which the history of the world has been so long filled. They may be shewn to have been neither foreseeing nor able in their methods, whether of resistance or concession to the new-born spirit; but it is unjust to set them down as its intractable adversaries. In the formidable strife of our day between governments and revolutions, history will surely not impute to the former the most insolent contempt of justice and liberty. And if the spirit of revolution were as moderate in its pretensions and acts, as governments have shown themselves disposed to be towards the spirit of progress, the great problem of the conciliation of order and liberty, in civil society, would be near its solution.

The government of religious society, or to speak with greater accuracy and freedom, the Catholic Church, has an analogous problem to solve; the more important because if the state of the minds of men is closely watched, it is seen that it is in the religious order that the idea of liberty is strongest and most deeply rooted. The right of conscience before God appears and is, in fact, very superior to that of conscience before men. If there be, in the life of the soul, one portion in which the intervention of force is more than elsewhere unrighteous and odious, it is clearly when the relation of the soul with her Creator and Judge is in question, and when the question for her is of eternity and salvation. Here, moreover, is a feeling which we have all experienced, a principle to which we have all paid homage. Christians or philosophers, Catholics or Protestants, we have all had and still have, even amidst the most civilized nations, need to invoke in our turn religious liberty, as that which, of all the cries for liberty, most surely arouses in the heart the idea of a sacred right and necessity, that which excites the most lively susceptibility and most general sympathy.

I feel a profound respect for the Catholic Church. She has been during centuries the Christian Church of all Europe. She is the great Christian Church of France. I look upon her dignity, her liberty, her moral authority, as essential to the fate of entire Christianity; and did I believe that the Catholic church could not, without self-abjuration, accept in the State the principle of religious liberty, I should be silent; for above all things I detest hypocrisy and subtlety. **But it is not so**.

Let the Catholic Church maintain fully her fundamental principles, her permanent inspiration, her doctrinal infallibility, her unity. Let her by her laws and internal discipline interdict to her faithful followers all that may tend to the injury of these; it is her right as well as her faith. But let her at the same time fully admit, not of the separation of the Church and State, that clumsy expedient which lowers and weakens both under the pretext of freeing both, but of the separation of spiritual and temporal order, of the civil and religious state, and acknowledge the illegality of all forcible interference in spiritual order, albeit in the cause of truth. Let her thus accept religious liberty as a law, not of religious society, but of policy, as a right not of the Christian, but of the citizen. At once will the pretended incompatibility between modern society and the Catholic Church disappear. The problem of peace between civil and religious society will be solved.

The Catholic Church can pursue this course; for all that religiously constitutes it, all her spiritual order thus remains intact and independent: and if she so pursues it; if, while she firmly upholds her principles and rights as a religious society, she accepts loyally the principles of our political order and the religious liberty which forms a part of it; not only will she lay the foundation of peace between herself and civil society, but she will assure to herself great strength and a great future. Christianity has many conquests to make and to repeat. For the re-establishment of social order and the moral welfare of the soul, she must regain much ground. Nor is it known how rapidly obstacles and resistance would disappear before her, if the dread of her old intolerance were dispelled, and respect for religious liberty on the part of the Catholic Church herself considered as assured.

I would go still further, and submit to Christians another consideration.

There is amongst Christians of whatever church a common faith. They believe in a divine revelation contained in the gospels, and in Jesus Christ who came upon earth to save the world.

For Christians of whatever church there is now a common cause. They have to maintain Christian faith and law against impiety and anarchy.

This faith and this necessity, common to all Christians, are of infinitely greater moment than all the differences which separate them.

Do I say that they ought at all hazards to set aside those differences, and in the name of their common faith and common danger undergo fusion,—

to use an expression of the day,—and form hereafter but one and the same church?

I do not dream of it. The re-establishment of unity in the bosom of Christianity by the re-union of all Christian churches, has been the desire and the endeavour of the greatest minds, both Catholic and Protestant. Bossuet and Leibnitz have attempted it. Even now the idea is present to many noble spirits, and pious bishops have so expressed it to me, with a confidence by which I feel profoundly honoured. I respect the sympathetic wish, but I do not believe that it can be realised. Between temporal order and human interests, fusion, difficult as it may be, is always possible; for interests may be made to agree through the force and in the name of necessity. In spiritual order and between religious beliefs, no such agreement is possible, for necessity can never become truth. Faith does not admit of fusion; she insists on unity.

But where the unity of the church does not exist, when the fusion of different churches is impossible, and when religious liberty is established, there is room for practical good sense and Christian charity. Good sense tells Christians that they are all in front of the same enemy, much more dangerous to them than they can be to each other; for should he triumph, the blow will fall on each. Amongst the upper classes, the war against religion manifests itself only under the forms of reserved scepticism or rationalism; timid, often serious and polite, rather seeking to screen than display itself. But at the bottom of society, and amidst the masses, it is passionate impiety which is at work, and for the sake of victory becomes subservient to the most gross and furious interests. The Christian faith, in its essential and vital character, that is, faith and submission to supernatural Christian order, is alone capable of sustaining the contest. Let Christians, whether Catholic or Protestant, be convinced of it, the loss of credit and authority on either side would redound to the advantage not of Protestantism or Catholicism, but of impiety. It is then for all Christians, whatever their differences in their Christian sphere, an obvious interest and imperative duty to accept and maintain each other as natural allies against anti-christian impiety. It will require all their strength, all their united efforts, to triumph finally in this warfare, and save at once Christianity and society.

What interest dictates to Christians, Christian charity commands. I use without hesitation plain words to express the ideas and sentiments which I feel, and even amidst the coldness of heart which is one of the most melancholy evils of my day, I feel no embarrassment in speaking to Christians of Christian charity.

When religious struggles are the ruling passion and great practical business of an epoch,—when different creeds are arrayed, wielding temporal as well as spiritual arms, with the mutual hope of subjecting if not of extirpating,—I feel that Christian charity is difficult to exercise. The temptations are too strong, the interests too pressing to be surmounted. The Chancellor De L'Hopital and the President De Thou, though recommending peace to Catholics and Protestants, would hardly have dreamt, on the eve or the morrow of a massacre or a battle, of speaking to them of charity.

But when material strife has ceased, when religious liberty is established in manners as well as in the laws, when in fact and truth the different religious creeds are obliged to live peaceably one with another, why should not the desire arise of adorning and furthering peace by the exercise of charity? When the coarser passions are powerless, why should not the more mild and equitable feelings develope themselves? I know the force of traditions, of recollections, as well as the permanent differences which tend to support controversy, even when purely speculative. Nevertheless, prolonged peace and freedom have much influence in calming the soul. At this day we have before us a signal instance, and I do not hesitate to repeat that to which I gave utterance in the Bible Society: —"See what is passing in England; there, doubtless, the irritation of the Protestants is great, there is a general and passionate movement in favour of a popular and powerful faith. The government itself associates with and follows this movement. English Protestantism shows itself strongly inclined to seek security and satisfaction at the expense of the religious liberty of the Catholics. Well! although matters wear this appearance, nothing is really done; they dare not; they cannot; and in the bottom of their hearts they desire not to do so. Amidst this Protestant excitement, the religious liberty of English Catholics still remains and extends. They have liberty of worship; their churches are open, nay, increasing in number;

their priests perform their duties without interruption: they possess the liberty of the press; they publicly defend their creed and their conduct, and have freedom of speech and power of voting in parliament, where they strenuously uphold their cause." A noble sight, which, after having justly filled the friends of religious liberty with uneasiness, ought now to give them every satisfaction. The spirit of persecution had reappeared, that of justice and liberty met it face to face, and in spite of appearances remained master of the field. May Christians, Catholic and Protestant, at last acknowledge it; it will be hereafter more natural than they imagine, to live in the exercise of Christian charity, for they have lost the habit, almost the power of efficacious oppression.

A few words more, and I have done. Under a well grounded and well understood system of religious freedom, not only can different religious sects live peacefully and harmoniously together, but can contribute, by their pacific co-existence, to their mutual religious prosperity. What has been for Catholicism in France one of the most glorious and pious periods? Surely, the seventeenth century. French Catholicism then flourished in the presence of Protestantism, which was still tolerated, and Jansenism, then in full vigour. What has prevented the Anglican church from falling into that apathy which has appeared more than once ready to overcome her? What but the neighbourhood of opposing and half free sects, who have always kept her in play, and forced her to overcome her langour? There is no establishment, no power, that is not benefited by a sense of control, and by the necessity of making an effort to maintain its position. It is good to overcome, not to exterminate an enemy; and in spiritual as in temporal orders, the reign of liberty bestows on all their just rewards. While it preserves their rights to the weak, it incessantly regenerates the victorious.

Doubtless, Catholicism leans on the principle of authority; but without detaching itself from this base, it can admit, and in the course of its career has often admitted, very different degrees of liberty. From the eleventh to the fourteenth century, while the Catholic church was for civil society a great school of authority, she was in her own bosom a great theatre of freedom. For in her councils, her congregations, her correspondence with the faithful, discussion between her chiefs was ever open and animated. It is not for me to ask whether our times advise or warrant a return to such methods of government; and I am rather disposed to hesitate than undertake the task. But one great fact strikes me; one which deserves, if I mistake not, the entire attention of the Catholic clergy: it is that the disposition of the mind and heart of the faithful who are under their charge is not always the same, and neither the same measure nor the same quality of religious nutriment is requisite at all times, if I may so speak, for Christian souls. After the fall of the Roman empire, when the mission of the Catholic clergy was to convert the barbarians, and to cause a little moral light to penetrate amongst the rude conquerors, and the miserable population who lived under their yoke, it was above all by the firm and striking exercise of religious authority that the priests were enabled to attain their end. They found amongst the Christian population, high and low, many passions to repress, and but few intellectual wants to satisfy. There was greater need to strike and to govern the imagination than to nourish and direct mental activity. Time and individuals are now different. Minds are now active, varied, curious, eager. The spiritual life of faithful Christians, of the most faithful as well as the most wavering, is infinitely more animated than it was formerly. Souls so disposed require a moral rule proportionably animated; one which, while it guides, may give to their innate activity a greater share of satisfaction. I am expressing a profound conviction,—one, I will venture to say, free from any reservation or ill-will,—when I say that henceforth the Catholic church, without any sacrifice of authority, will be obliged, for the government of the soul, to admit of more intellectual and spontaneous movement on the part of the faithful than was required in other times. Yet I am convinced that when once the Catholic church shall herself have acknowledged this new moral state of Christian society, she will also know how to provide for it.

In a recent publication, [Footnote 1] a justly eminent stranger, M. Donoso Cortes, speaking of me in terms which I cannot allow myself to repeat, said, "The great mistake into which M. Guizot has fallen, in his 'History of European Civilization,' is the having attempted the impossible task of explaining visible things by visible things, natural things by natural things; which is as superfluous as to explain a fact by itself, a thing by the thing itself; because all visible and natural things, considered as visible and natural, are one and the same thing."

[Footnote 1: Essai sur le Catholicisme, le Liberalisme, et le Socialisme, par M. Donoso Cortes, Marquis de Valdegamas, p. 99-105.]

M. Donoso Cortes will be convinced, I hope, that such is not my idea; and that, far from resting satisfied with visible and natural things, I believe in supernatural order, and in its necessity to explain and govern the world. Philosophers, I think, will on their side acknowledge that if I reject their doctrine, I do not abandon their right. I do not say this with the view of seeking the frivolous honour of maintaining at the same time two great causes, but to affirm a double truth to which I yield my entire conviction and devotion, Christian faith and religious freedom. The welfare of all nations demands these as its price.

Guizot.

Val Richer, September, 1851.

On The State Of Men's Souls.
(*October*, 1838.)

The sublimity of the gospel consists in two sentiments, which manifest themselves in it simultaneously,—hatred of evil, and tenderness for man who does evil; horror of sin, to speak as the gospel speaks, and love of the sinner.

How profound a depth of judgment as well as of moral justice! How admirable a knowledge of things as well as of men! For evil is truly hateful both in itself and in its effects; and men, the best of men, are surcharged with evil. Yet, at the same time, man is infinitely capable of good, infinitely worthy of affection; and with all his imperfections, a being to be loved beyond expression.

How great, too, the knowledge displayed of the true conditions of moral authority! It is not acquaintance with the nature of man, but power over him, that the Gospel seeks. Yet to influence men morally, it is needful both to love and reform them; to win their confidence by love and their respect by severity. Severity and love are the two engines wherewith to control the heart of man, for men know by instinct their moral wants—those which press them down as well as those which please them. They are deeply troubled by the sense of their imperfections; they wish to be raised. Love felt and inspired is at once their noblest and their most lively joy; they desire to love and be beloved. Complete control over them, I mean moral control, involves these two conditions,—that much be required from them of virtue, much be bestowed on them of love.

The last century had thus much good; it loved mankind and men. It bore a really deep affection to them, and wished them well. But as it was a critical and reasoning age, the sentiment of love often disguised itself in the dress and shape of controversy and analysis. Nevertheless, the feeling was there, sincere and powerful. That spirit of universal justice and humanity which characterized the epoch, whence did it spring if not from a lively sympathy with man, and a tender interest in his welfare?

But, together with this virtue, the last century certainly exhibited one great defect; it did not feel for evil the aversion it deserves. Not only as regarded certain rules of conduct and certain duties, but as concerned a rule in general and the very principle of duty, the spirits of the day were victims to doubt, that great corrupter of the human heart. In the moral system, stability and elevation go together; to waver is to descend; uncertainty is the sign and the cause of abasement. Not knowing where the evil existed, or even if it did exist, the eighteenth century denied or excused it when met with, instead of execrating and opposing it to the utmost.

And with the fixed points the long perspectives disappeared. By an admirable law of his nature, in order that man may hope he must believe, and believe in good. Virtue alone demands an eternity. Doubting about duty, they doubted their own future. Moral faith tottered; God veiled his countenance.

In such a state of mind, in an age which loved man and interested itself about him, man must have been an object of pity. What a destiny was that of a creature thus powerful yet faltering; always in motion, yet not knowing where to fix his foot firmly in this world, or where to fix his gaze beyond it! To aspire so high, in order to fall low and pass away so quickly! Such ambition without a worthy object! Such labour without any sure results! What father, if he thought his child were reserved for such a lot, but would feel overwhelmed by compassion and grief?

But no! at the same time that the last century loved men it admired them; and I can understand this. God and duty being abandoned, what remains of great and good if it be not man? Imperfect as is human nature, a mixture of good and evil, good is found there; the power of good makes itself felt. All that it possesses of what is elevated, rich, tender, or attractive, does not necessarily vanish because the mind misunderstands its source and government. And if it should happen, as it then did, that these great mental errors should occur in the midst of a period of great intellectual developement, of a great outflowing of sympathetic and noble sentiments, of a great march in the condition of mankind; if, at the moment when man rises highest and shines with most brilliancy, he loses sight of his compass, his God, how can he do otherwise than admire himself? how avoid a feeling of pride? He has no longer faith or hope on high, yet he advances, prospers, becomes rich, triumphs. He must believe; he must hope in himself; he must worship himself. Does religion fall? Then idolatry must arise, the idolatry of man for man. Man was the god of the eighteenth century, the object of worship as well as of love. Thence a great and deplorable leaning to human nature, to its weaknesses and inclinations. It was loved, but with a blind and weak love, which could only approve, caress, and promise, having nothing to advise, nothing to require.

Thence an immoderate thirst, in the name of and for man, of immediate worldly and palpable happiness. Loving man truly, and having nothing to offer him in this world superior to this world's happiness, nothing better or eternal beyond, it was necessary that men should be happy, that all should be happy here below; as here below their destiny and their treasure were contained. To accept the imperfect condition of humanity may be the part of selfishness which cares for nothing, and of faith which hopes for everything; but he who loves men, and yet can only dispose in their favour the blessings of this life and this world, cannot resign himself to a lot for the most part so rude, to progress so slow and always so incomplete. He is compelled to find much more to bestow on men, to distribute something, and at once, to all. And as spirits imbued with so noble a longing do not dream of the impossibility of satisfying it, they are compelled to assign to the sufferings and hardships of the human state an accidental and factitious cause, one which human wisdom and power can overcome. Hence the other maxim of the last century, that, left to themselves and their natural equilibrium, men and things go on well; that evil proceeds not from our innate nature and state, but merely from the ill regulated state of society, where the few have substituted their will and interest for the wills and interests of the many; that it is society and not men that need reformation, as the latter would not need it had not society corrupted him.

A maxim which has given rise, and naturally, to the sorest and most plausible of modern grievances, that incurable impatience of whatever is, that boundless disquiet, that insatiable thirst for change in the pursuit of a social condition which shall give at last to man, to every man, all the happiness to which he aspires.

This is the state in which the eighteenth century has placed men's souls. And I here speak of upright, honest, and sincere minds, not carried away by selfishness, not domineered over by evil passions, which think of others, and only wish for themselves as well as for those others what they consider legitimate.

The great mistakes and ills of any epoch are those of the good. These must be looked to and provided against, for there lies the hidden danger. Who can struggle against ill if the good are themselves infected with it?

I have seen the last of the master spirits of the eighteenth century—those who had remained faithful to it. I have seen them emerging from our revolution after their fearful experience of it. The condition of their minds was a touching and instructive spectacle. They were sorrowful, but not discouraged; full of esteem and affection for mankind; full of confidence and hope despite so many mistakes and reverses. The same fertility of wit, the same generosity of heart, the same spirit of justice and progress animated them. They accounted for their momentary failure by the violence of passion, the force of old habits, the want of public intelligence, the too hasty application of good principles carried to too great a length. And while their explanation bore witness to their sincerity and perseverance, still there was visible and perceptible in them at every step a persistance in the same mistakes; the same absence of moral dogma and religious faith; the same idolatry of man, the same tenderness towards him, the same pretensions for him. They had lost nothing of their noble ambition or tender sympathy for human nature, but they had learned nothing of its inward laws nor of the true methods for its government.

Thus a secret feeling of disquiet was apparent through the constancy of their ideas and of their hope; and they remained melancholy after their explanation, as if hardly satisfied with it themselves.

We are far in advance of our fathers. "I was carried here by a cannon shot," said Danton to M. de Talleyrand, who saw him at the Ministere de la Justice. The same shot has carried us all a hundred leagues from our cradle. We have learnt much. We have seen novel appearances under a new light. The intelligence and power of man; his reason, his morality, his power of action, and resistance to direction and restraint in the affairs of the world; all has been put to the proof, gauged, and measured. We know how deeply seated and closely hidden is the evil in our nature, yet how readily and terribly it occasionally breaks out. We know the bounds both of our spirit and of our will. We have been powerful, immensely powerful; and yet we have been unable to accomplish our will because it was in opposition to the laws of eternal wisdom, and our power was shivered against them like glass. At this price, we have acquired a more accurate and profound knowledge of ourselves and our condition. We no longer put ourselves off with desires or arguments, appearances or hopes. We see that which is. We live more than our fathers did in the truth. We are wiser and more modest.

But our wisdom has one grave defect. It is still, if I may so speak, but an outward good, which influences our life and conduct, but has not yet penetrated our soul and become for us a moral property, a moral wealth. It redounds to the honour and greatness of man that he is not content with what *is*, merely because it is. The mere fact does not suffice; he wishes to see more. For the fact he would discover an end, a reason. He wishes to attach it to the laws of his own inward nature, his own destiny; to feel it in relation to and harmony with his soul. Then only in man's eyes does a fact assume a moral aspect and acquire a moral power; then only does man accept it and obey it with respect as truth, instead of yielding and submitting to it with pain as a necessity. Moreover, we do not yet understand all the lessons of experience which we have received and recognized. They have not yet assumed in our moral being the rank which belongs to them. They are for us unimpeachable facts rather than great and good laws; and mistakes rather than progress. They direct more than they have enlightened us, and if we conform our actions and thoughts to them, it is because we are subdued rather than convinced.

Were it not so, why this dejection, this secret disgust, this indifference, this bluntness, this chill which now so often accompany wisdom and sound sense? You say you are discouraged, you do not hope, you do not dare any more to attempt aught that is difficult and great. What then has happened? What has this experience, at the same time so much vaunted and so mournful, taught you? That duty, not interest or passion, is the principle of morality; that God has not ceased to watch over the world; that he resists the proud and punishes the guilty; that order has her natural and inviolable laws, and avenges herself on those who mistake them; that evil, always present, always at our door, in us and about us, needs to be incessantly resisted. Of what do you complain? These are advances, not mistakes; truths reconquered, power recovered, not hopes thrown away. It is true, man was carried away by an ambition beyond his strength and right; it must be brought down, his reason and his will must agree to restore what they attempted to usurp. Instead of setting up and adoring himself as a monarch, man here must acknowledge his primitive imperfection, his definite insufficiency, and yield submission in thought and life on the bosom of liberty. But is it nothing that this liberty is now more firmly established than man has ever known it? Is the general progress of justice and happiness in the world nothing? Is there not therein a fitting reward for the toils and sufferings of our age? Is there not, after so many mistakes, enough to satisfy the most exacting, to refresh the most exhausted?

Let us look higher. In return for the sacrifices required from our pride, in compensation for the demonstrated weakness of our nature and the marked bounds of our power, has nothing been given to us? Do we not regain more than we lose? Do we not ascend more than we have been forced to descend? The eighteenth century had inflated us with pride, yet had in reality only lowered us. In making us monarchs of this world, it had at the same time confined and reduced us to it alone. No more immensity, no more eternity for the soul; no longer a bond of kindred between God and man. We came and passed over the earth like all that springs from and returns to it. Our noblest ambition, our purest desires, our most sublime flights, all that there is in us of noble and truly divine, was no more than a delusion and a burden. Not only in respect of our worldly goods and joys, but of ourselves and for ever, we had to exclaim, "vanity of vanities, all is vanity." We have escaped; we are leaving this confined and low condition; we are rising; we are again about to attain our dignity, our hope, our futurity, our soul. We can no more parade ourselves in our pride, but we are no longer plunged into and abandoned in misery; we find again a Master here below, and also "our Father which is in heaven."

I know how much there is of the frivolous and superficial in the return of our time to religious hopes and beliefs. I know how much even serious minds are doubtful and agitated upon this subject, the evils that are still at work, the problems that await solution, and that perhaps a tardy one. Nevertheless, we have got back to the right track. Man does not increase his distance from God; he has turned towards the East; he seeks the light. Here we still yield rather to the force of facts than of ideas; and experience is credited rather than conviction. Still we believe in experience rather than in our own talent, and submit to facts though we hardly render a free and enlightened homage to the truths of which they witness.

It is not yet adoration, but it is the fear of God, that beginning of wisdom.

Had we already reached the point of adoration—were the wisdom for which we have so dearly paid really established amongst us, in the affairs of this world and in those of eternity, in questions political, moral, and religious, in short, in everything; and were we fully satisfied as to the rational lawfulness and practical utility of her counsels, if she enlightened our understandings as she rules our conduct—we should be far other than we are; more tranquil, more confiding, more firm, more worthy, more exalted. We should distinguish further; we should advance higher and faster in the paths of new and amending progress, in which we now walk slowly and with bended head, as if constrained and humbled.

But, I repeat, it is needful, for this salutary transformation of our ideas to be accomplished, that our experience may become our reason. We have more good sense than enlightenment; we act better than we think. Inwardly and deeply we are imbued with prejudices which fetter although they do not rule us; we are still doubtful about the very truths by which we test our deeds; only doubt has changed its form and language. With our fathers it was infatuated and bold; with us it is detracting and useless.

Pride has turned it into contempt; and because we do not experience for human nature the unbounded ambition and chimerical hopes which formerly prevailed, we no longer love men tenderly, nor think well of their nature, nor take an interest in their destiny. We imagine that wisdom binds us to indifference and immobility.

Many, too, of the ills of the eighteenth century, which sprung from the maxims then prevalent, and which, to all appearance, ought to have expired with them, still exist. We no longer have the same tenderness for man, nor do we show greater aversion to evil. Indifference has not made us more strict. For though human nature is no longer judged with the same blind partiality, we are still full of indulgence towards it, and cowardly in our treatment of it; we exhibit towards it the same complaisance, without feeling the former esteem and love. Materialist and impious doctrines are on the decline, but we are more than ever tormented by an eager thirst for immediate material happiness.

Is it true then, as is said, that we are in a state of moral decay? Is our age destined to continue the evil of its precursor, and while losing its virtues add to it its own evils?

I confidently answer in the negative. Nothing would tempt me to flatter the age I live in, but I love it. I am struck by its evil; I think a remedy urgently called for, an immediate struggle necessary; I also see in it much good, a good deep and fruitful and sufficient with the help of God to resist and conquer the evil.

I said just now that the great mistakes, the serious maladies of any period are those of the good. On the other side, it is in the sound ideas and good dispositions of the same class that the moral force of an epoch and its means of safety are to be found. Now the general and ruling disposition of the good at the present day is the spirit of order, the deep desire for order after so much trouble and contest.

This is said to be merely the result of prudence, of a clear idea of interest, not of morality.

In my opinion this is an inconsiderate sentence; one which shows little knowledge of man and of what passes within him, of which he is often himself unconscious. There is morality, true morality, in the spirit of order, especially when largely developed and hardly tried. The word ***interest*** is pronounced disdainfully, as if it implied pure selfishness, and excluded virtue. Thanks be to God, who has created legitimate interests. Interests inherent to legitimate situations and relations are essentially moral and animated by moral impulsion. The father of a family who protects his household, the labourer who takes care of the fruit of his industry, act for their own interest it is true, and according to the dictates of prudence. But around and connected with this interest are grouped the most praiseworthy feelings, domestic affections, respect of the law, care for the future, defence of right, fulfilment of duty, efforts, devotion, sacrifice. Who will refuse to these the name of morality? Public instinct answers this question. "There are but two parties," said a man of simple mind, and a stranger to all sophism, "that of honest men and that of rogues." When it was desired to define and rally under one banner the party of order in France, it was inscribed "The Charter and Property." [Footnote 2]

    [Footnote 2: "La Charte et les gens de bien."]

In fact, at the present day the ideas of honesty, dignity, morality, and virtue are closely allied with that of order. Public morality is in the general mind the cause of order as well as of individual security. It is because, after so many convulsions as corrupt as painful, the taste for and love of order are amongst us the first effect, the first symptom of attachment to the maxims and practice of duty.

Besides, democratic societies, still so novel and mysterious, are little known and ill understood. Their virtues want the éclat,—I will go further, want the finish, the charm which belong to the elevation of persons, the beauty of form, the influence of time, the complete, varied and harmonious developement of great and glorious human nature. Yet they want neither virtue itself nor morality. There will be found in these crowded and unknown masses, in their laborious and modest lives, much uprightness, much simple justice, much active benevolence, much submission to law, much resignation to their lot, a rare power of effort and sacrifice, a noble and touching disposition to forgetfulness of self, without pretension, without noise, without reward.

Even the jealousy of all superiority, the passion of envy—that poison of democratic society,—does not always affect as much as might be apprehended their moral judgment. This venom has affected us deeply; nevertheless, excellence is met with joy and welcomed with gratitude as a service done to society, which feels the necessity of being elevated and purified. Respect is more genuine, taste more correct while it remains a stranger to systematic opinions, to mere flights of fancy, and to all romantic emphasis. By a singular and very significant phenomenon, the exaggeration and emphasis of the present period tend towards evil and disorder. The declaimer plunges into the mire. Our times wish good to be true, simple, sedate, and sensible. It is only because it is good, a moral good, that it is esteemed and loved. It is asked to appear but what it is.

Where such a disposition prevails; where good is thus honored for itself, and for itself alone, there may still be much evil, and very serious evil; but such can hardly be the lot of the future.

We are hardly yet advancing towards a future. As yet we have struggled, and still strive to acquire from the heritage of the last century a spoil that suits us; a heritage so loaded, so mingled, that it has plunged us in confusion. We have co-existing in us good and bad, true and false, in direct opposition. We bear about in ourselves the most contradictory ideas and sentiments. We are driven about and stagger under their varying influence. Now we try to reject all absolutely, now to forget all and live from day to day without thought or design. Vain efforts! The problem harasses every soul, agitates or wearies it, leaves it in doubt or inactivity. None can elude it. A solution is necessary in moral as well as in political order, for individuals as for the state. For this is not a purely political question, which can be settled wholly and completely by charter, law, or cabinet. It is a matter which comes home to each of us; one for which each of us individually has to provide. We must keep, apart from the impulse which the eighteenth century has given to the world and the minds of men, that which agrees with the eternal order which that era often mistook for the world and the human mind. The new truths and laws which come to us from that date, as well as the immutable truths and laws which it overlooked, must live and reign together in our thoughts; we must know for a certainty and unhesitatingly practice what they demand from us. On this condition only shall we see the end of that mixture of agitation and depression, this doubting both of well and ill regulated minds, this barrenness of movement as of wisdom which are the peculiar evils of our era. Government and people reciprocally accuse each other of this evil, and charge on each other the task of applying a remedy. "Let Power be dignified, firm, active, fertile," says the one; "let it sustain and animate, rule and aid society; society will assist, evils will be remedied, good will be done; but it is for Power to take the initiative and responsibility in all this." "How can I do it?" replies Power. "How undertake the responsibility? It is in society itself—in the mind itself—that the evil exists. They are weak, tottering, inactive; full of doubts and fears. Let people ascend in the social scale; let them show self-control. I do not prevent them. No one can ask me to do more; I can do no more."

The defence of both weakness of mind and heart is bad. The regeneration of our time demands from all both duty and exertion. From power, because it is set on high, it sees and is seen; it shows the light and holds the standard. If it lowers them, society falls into darkness and disorder. From society too, from every individual, for we are all infected by the evil which we call upon power to cure. Yet power of itself is not able to cure, individually and collectively, the evils for which we ask a remedy. Our active and intelligent co-operation is indispensible. And it is precisely in this coalition of public power and individual will that the value and honor of free governments consist. Hence they are morally and politically powerful, salutary for immortal souls as for temporal occasions.

This good must be the work of all. Power or society, rulers or plain citizens, let us each look to our own share in the great work, and perform our own part of the general duty. To him who shall be able the best and speediest to fulfil his, will belong the glory as well as the power inherent to success.

On Religion In Modern Societies.

(*February*, 1838.)

It is the fashion of the day loudly to lament over the condition of that great mass—the people. Their wants and sufferings are paraded. We are told of their lives so burdened and monotonous, so rude and precarious, so much fatigue, yet so little effect, so much danger and ennui, work so heavy, repose so slight, a future so uncertain.

This is true. The condition of the masses in this world is neither easy, cheerful, nor certain. It is impossible to contemplate without deep commiseration so many human creatures carrying, from their cradle to their tomb, so grievous a burden, and withal scarcely able to meet their wants, the wants of their children, of their father, their mother; incessantly seeking some necessary of life for those most dear, yet not always finding it; having it perhaps to-day, uncertain of it tomorrow; and continually preoccupied about their material existence, scarcely able to give a thought to their moral being. It is painful, most painful to witness, most painful to reflect on. Yet is much reflection necessary. It were a grievous wrong and a grievous danger to forget it. More or less thought has been ever given to the subject. What said they who thought the most thereon?

They advised those who were the fortunate of this world to practise justice, goodness, charity; to apply themselves to seeking out and relieving the unhappy. To the unfortunate they recommended good conduct, moderate desires, submission to authority, resignation, and hope. They explained the destiny of man, showed all it possesses of sadness and sublimity, the compensations which are found in the different states, the pleasures which are common to all. They tried to cure, amongst the ills of men, those which men can cure; and, with regard to those which are incurable here below, they strove to raise men's eyes to the remedies in

God's hands. This was the language of religion. These were the words and advice she addressed to high and low, rich and poor, to children in her catechisms, to men in her sermons, from the pulpit and from the sanctuary, by the sick bed, to all, at all seasons, and by every means.

The means of publicity and popular movement at that time belonged almost exclusively to religion. What the tribune, the press, the post—these trumpets of modern civilization—now are, the churches, the pulpit, religious instruction, pastoral superintendence formerly were Religion then addressed the masses. She never forgot the people. She was ever able to gain access there.

And while she thus interested herself for them, and strove to lighten or partly bear the burden of life, she also sympathised with men of all classes and all conditions, and with the burdens all bear, the blows which reach all, the wounds which all receive as they tread their appointed path.

To-day, while occupying ourselves much and justly with the material sufferings and fatigue which are shared by so many, we forget too much the moral fatigues and sufferings of which all partake; the trials, the agonies of the soul, the mistakes, the ennui, the anguish, in short, the universal lot of man—which are the more poignant as the mind has more freedom and life more leisure.

High or low, rich or poor, the *elite* or the multitude, let us pity each other, let us pity every one. We are all, as we advance in our career, "weary and heavy laden"; we all deserve pity.

We deserve it now more than ever. Never, it is true, has the condition of man been more equal or better. But the desires of men have far outrun their progress. Never was ambition more impatient and widespread. Never were so many hearts a prey to the thirst for wealth and pleasure. Pleasures refined and grovelling, a thirst of material well-being and of intellectual variety, a spirit of activity and luxury, of adventure and idleness: everything appears possible, desirable, and accessible to all. It is not that passion is strong, or that man is disposed to take much trouble for the gratification of his desires. He wishes feebly, desires immoderately; and the great scope of his desire throws him into a state of uneasiness, in which all that he already possesses appears but as the drop of water forgotten as soon as swallowed, and which irritates thirst instead of quenching it. The world has never seen such a conflict of imperfect desires, fancies, pretensions, exactions; never heard such a clamour of voices demanding together as their right all they have not and all that pleases them.

And these voices are not raised to God. Ambition, is at once extended and debased. When the teachers of the people were religious preceptors, they tried to detach the popular thought from the things of earth, and by raising desires and hopes to heaven, to restrain and calm them here. They knew that here, do what they might, satisfaction was impossible. The popular teachers of this day think otherwise and speak another language. In the presence of the hard lot and burning ambition of man, at the very time that they are displaying their misery and fomenting their desires, they are telling them that this earth contains what will satisfy them; and that if each be not as happy as he would be, it is not in the nature of things nor of his own nature that he should complain, but of the vices of society, and the usurpations of a certain class of men. All are placed in this world to be happy; all have the same right to happiness; the world can afford happiness to all.

Words like these resound daily in the ears of all, knock at the portals of every heart, penetrate by every crevice into the most remote folds of society.

And then we are astonished at the deep agitation and uneasiness under which nations and individuals, states and souls are labouring! For myself, I wonder the uneasiness is not greater, the agitation more violent, the explosion more sudden. Such ideas and such words are enough to set humanity astray and rouse it to revolt. And the preserving care of Providence, the innate and spontaneous wisdom which men cannot absolutely shake off, must be powerful to prevent such language— unceasingly repeated and universally heard—from plunging the world again into chaos.

No, it is not true that this earth possesses that which will suffice for the ambition and happiness of her inhabitants. It is not true that the untoward results or vices of human institutions are the sole or even the principal causes of the sad and painful lot of so many among men. Let these institutions become daily more just, more careful of the general welfare; it is the right of mankind. It is to the honour of our age that it adopted this thought and perseveres in trying to accomplish it. Former times took too light a share in the sufferings of the multitude. Their pretensions were too humble as regards justice and happiness for all. Ours are more extended, more lofty; and we give, with good reason, to our advance in this path the noble name of civilization. God forbid that we should turn aside from the noble work, or be discouraged about such a noble hope. But we must not feed ourselves with pride and illusion, we must not promise to ourselves that which we cannot expect to attain of ourselves and by our ingenuity. There is a defect in our nature and an evil in our condition which eludes all human efforts. The disorder is within ourselves, and were every other source dried up, would arise from ourselves and our own will. An inequality of suffering is amongst the providential laws of our destiny. It is at once superiority and infirmity, greatness and misery. As free beings, we can create and do in fact without ceasing create evil. As immortal beings, neither the secrets of our lot nor the limits of our ambition are on this earth, and the life we lead here is but a very short scene of the unknown life which awaits us. Regulate institutions as you will, distribute all enjoyment as you please, neither your wisdom nor your wealth will fill the abyss. The liberty of man is stronger than the institutions of society. The mind of man is greater than worldly goods. There will always be found in him more desires than social knowledge can regulate or satisfy, more sufferings than it can either prevent or cure.

"Religion, religion!" is the cry of universal man everywhere, at all times, except in some day of awful extremity or shameful degradation. Religion, to restrain or crown man's ambition. Religion, to sustain or support us in our griefs, whether referring to body or soul. Let not policy the most strong, the most just, flatter itself that it can effect this without religion. The greater and more extensive the social movement, the less able is it to direct tottering humanity. A higher power than any on earth is needed, a longer prospect than that of this life. God and eternity are necessary.

We require harmony also and agreement between religion and policy. Called to act on the same individual, and as a final attempt for the same result, how can they work together unless possessing a common basis of thought, sentiments, and designs? Whatever distance may intervene, there is an intimate connection between the earthly and religious ideas of men, between their desires for time and those for eternity. Did incoherence and contradiction alone exist, were our affairs, opinions, and hopes here completely estranged from those beyond this world, were religion capable only of improving and sustaining our actual life and society, their ideas, works, institutions and manners, far from serving the cause of, and mutually assisting each other would reciprocally fetter and weaken one another. The world would jest at piety, piety would take offence at the world, and that which should be upon earth the source of order and peace would become a fresh spring of anarchy and war.

And let neither religion or policy be alarmed about its independence and dignity. I do not wish that either should purchase by cowardly concession or costly sacrifice the harmony which ought to prevail between them. On the contrary, I wish they should on all occasions act according to the pure truth of things, and accomplish together their special and peculiar mission.

Clever men have looked upon religion as a source of order, a sort of social police, a useful and even indispensable matter, but otherwise without intrinsic value or any real and definite importance to the individual, unless to afford a chimerical satisfaction to certain weaknesses of the human mind and heart. Thence arises a superficial and hypocritical respect, which barely covers a disdainful coldness ill-calculated to resist any prolonged trial, which humiliates religion if she is content with it, or otherwise irritates and misleads her.

Great and religious men have in their turn looked on the world and the life of the world, either generally or at certain periods, as an evil in itself, an essential obstacle to the empire of divine laws, and to the accomplishment of our moral destiny. Hence the follies of ascetics and sectarians; hence, too, theocratic pretensions, pitiable mistakes of the spirit of religion, which has thus entered into hostility with human society, wishing now to flee from it, now to subdue it.

The errors on both sides are great and dangerous. Religious creeds seek to solve the fundamental problems of our nature and individual destiny. That is their first and chief design, greater even in their eyes than the maintenance of order in society. For this reason, and for this reason especially, respect is due to them; they deal with that which is most inward, most powerful, and most noble in man. And the policy which does not discern these facts, or discerning does not respectfully bow before them, shows itself futile, ignorant of the nature of man, incapable of guiding him at moments of importance.

On the other hand, this earth is not a place of banishment where man lives an exile. Society is not a scene of perdition, which a man must go through with disgust and terror. The earth is man's first country; God has placed him here. Society is the natural condition of man; God has made it for him. This world and social life do not bound our destiny; but it is in this world and by this social life that our destiny is begun and developed. We owe to society our assistance, given affectionately and respectfully, whatever the form of its organisation and the difficulties of our task. These forms and difficulties change with places and times, but they possess only a secondary importance, and make no change in the general condition or fundamental duty of man.

Religion, without being indifferent to what there is of true or false, good or bad, in the casual and variable part of the social world, attaches herself to what is essential and permanent, training men to go straight towards heaven beneath every sky and by every road.

It is the glory of Christianity to have been the first to place religion on this height, and in this the only religious point of view. And yet, neither reasons nor temptations were wanting at its origin, to make it denounce temporal society, and either separate from or declare war against it. Still it never dreamt of such a course. At the moment when the Christian faith restored to man his lost dignity and raised him to his forfeited position, she made herself liable for him without a murmur to slavery, despotism, iniquities, inequalities, incomparable miseries. Not one revolutionary intention or idea, to use a modern phrase, is to be traced near the cradle of Christianity. Christians in the name of their faith heroically resist persecution and tyranny, but they do not undertake to change the state of society or of mankind. They share in it, they adapt themselves to it, whatever its principles, forms, consequences. They do more. The world is old and corrupt; they denounce and vigorously resist its corruptions and vices: but they do not curse, they do not avoid the world. They view it with indignation yet with affection, with grief yet with hope. Rigid minds, ardent imaginations, take fright at the sight of the world, and fly to the deserts of the Thebais or retreat within the walls of a cloister. Brilliant apparitions are those who impress the minds of nations, and renew the well-nigh forgotten strife between austere and impure passions; but these are only exceptions in the history of Christianity, imposing and powerful indeed, but they do not characterise the Christian religion, do not predominate in it, do not constitute its essence and general tendency. Christianity has made monks, yet never was a religion less monkish. Never was a religion introduced into the world which entered more into it, more easily accommodated itself to it, to all its phases and all its facts. Opposed to this day in the very country which saw its birth, Christianity spreads to the east and west, to the north and south. It penetrates the old monarchies of Asia and the deep forests of Germany, the schools of Athens and of Rome, the wandering tribes of the desert; and nowhere does it disturb itself about traditions, institutions, governments; it allies itself and lives in peace with the most diverse societies. It knows that everywhere and amidst all the variety of social forms it can pursue its own work, that truly religious work, the regeneration and safety of the soul.

In later days, after a definite victory, amidst Roman ruins and barbarian chaos, through necessity as well as love of power, Christianity has sought and exercised a more direct and commanding influence over civil society; an influence sometimes salutary, sometimes opposed to the nature of things, and often injurious to religion itself. Yet taking things as a whole, and setting aside some remarkable deviations, the Christian Church has with admirable wisdom been a stranger, in her intercourse with the world, to all narrow and exclusive spirit; has never attached to any peculiar social *regime* her honor and destiny. She has lived in kindly and intimate relation with the most different governments, with social systems the most opposed, monarchy, republic, aristocracy, democracy. Here on a level with the state, there subordinate, elsewhere independent. Broad and varied in her internal organization, as called for by her external relations; always sedulous to maintain between social and religious life, between the ideas and feelings by which men hold to earth or ascend to heaven, that harmony by which heaven and earth both profit. In our days, owing to the course of events and reciprocal faults, this harmony has been profoundly affected. Religion and society have for some time ceased to comprehend and agree with each other. The ideas, sentiments, and interests which now prevail in temporal life are and have often been condemned and reproved in the name of those which pertain to eternal life. Religion sometimes pronounces her anathemas upon the new world, and keeps herself aloof from it. The world seems ready to abide by both anathema and separation.

The evil is immense; it is one which aggravates all our other ills, which takes from social order and private life their security and dignity, their repose and hope.

To cure this evil, to bring together the spirit of Christianity and the spirit of the age, the old religion and new society, to end their hostility, and to induce a mutual understanding and acceptance, is the origin of a work too little known, that called the "**Universite Catholique**" which its authors have continued for three years with the most praiseworthy perseverance.

Thanks be theirs; thanks to men so truly pious, so truly catholic, who cast over new society, over constitutional France, a glance so equitable and affectionate. This gleam of justice towards our day, this hope loudly declared that it will accept eternal truth and must not be cursed in her name, is a proof of high intelligence on their part. God forbid that with frivolous blindness we should soothe each other with flattery. Our society has gone astray more than once on the most important matters, and even while triumphant is smitten with a serious disorder. And yet our time is a great time, which has done great things and opened great destinies. This society, so stormy, so confused, so tottering, sometimes so chimerical and arrogant, sometimes so material and grovelling, has nevertheless done homage and lent force to that which is most elevated and divine within us, our intelligence and justice. Much truth is contained in the motto of her banner; and wishing that this truth might be efficacious; she has displayed, in order to make it penetrate into deeds, an energy and ability which have astonished the world and drawn it after her. Such boldness of conception, such power of execution, such a development of mind, of passion, of strength, so many results positive and visible obtained rapidly, the general progress of happiness, wealth, and order, of practical and plain justice in social relations and affairs,—is there nought here but error? Are these the symptoms of decline? Do we not rather recognise one of those formidable but beneficial crises brought on by providence when desirous to renew the world? Proclaim without reserve to society the evil it has done, the evil it is undergoing; point out in all their extent and gravity its errors, its faults, its omissions, its weaknesses, its excesses, its crimes; but do not expect her to yield to injustice or wrong. She knows what she is and what she may become. The good she has devised, the good she has done to mankind, she would have honoured and loved. On these terms only will she redress and direct. She is in the right. One must seek for, listen to, and trust severe though stern friends. Confidence should never be placed in an enemy.

I do not think that the authors of **l'Université Catholique** render to society all the justice it deserves; but they have no concealed ill-will to it, no design against it. They understand and admit the essential principles upon which it is founded, and they try seriously and sincerely to re-establish between these principles and catholic doctrines, a harmony which shall not be merely superficial and apparent. Their plan is simple. After having traced a general outline of human sciences, together with the ties which unite them either among themselves or to the sublime unity to which they tend, they place therein special courses for each different science of material as of intellectual order, and try in those courses how to make religion penetrate into science, how science into religion, keeping both in sight, so that they may recognise, approach, and unite with each other in their common progress; consequently their body is a dumb university, where all science is taught by writings according to and in a catholic spirit, as they would be *viva voce* at a real university, where all the professors would be Catholics, truly devoted to their faith and their science.

I have no design of entering into the scientific merits of these courses, or of disputing all their assertions and ideas. Some, as the "Course of introduction to the study of Christian Truths," by M. l'Abbe Gerbet; the "Course on Christian Art," by M. Rio; the "Course on the General History of Hebrew Literature," by M. de Cazelès; contain real instruction, elevated and ingenious views, and sometimes rare talent in style, and much attraction for the reader. In a literary review joined to these "Courses" one finds occasional articles, amongst others those by M. le Comte de Montalembert, full of curious research and noble sentiments; written too with a moral earnestness which pleases and touches, even when it goes beyond what is true. It would be easy to collect from the entire work sufficiently numerous traces of superficial science, somewhat vague philosophy, or declamatory literature. I might here and there detect, and this is more important, some traces of old habits, and of that old spirit of hostility from which the authors of the collection have in general tried to keep themselves clear. Possibly, had I the honor of seeing them, I might venture in the freedom of conversation to urge them to weigh carefully in this respect their sentiments and language, to preserve constantly between their ideas and expressions, agreement with the general intentions which animate them and at which they aim. Let them be in this sense strict censors of their own work. As for me, I cannot be one; I cannot seek underhand means as regards the execution of a great and just idea to which I wish success. I admit of incompleteness and imperfection, even incoherency in a human work, provided it be in itself good, and that good predominates in its effects as well as intentions. The pleasure of criticism is mean; and for my own part I feel none in pointing out faults which I should like to efface.

I prefer congratulating the authors of **l'Université Catholique** on the firmness and fidelity with which they have remained faithful to their name and standard. In their excellent design, and on account of the conciliatory spirit which pervaded it, they encountered a shoal under their prow. They ran the danger of being induced to become effeminate and enervated, to pervert their own doctrines, the Catholic doctrines and spirit, in order to render their accommodation more in accordance with the ideas and spirit of the age. More than once analogous attempts, conceived in the best intentions, have split on this rock. It is thus that we have heard applied to natural religion and the general spirit of religion; these maxims that the dogma is of little consequence, the moral only being of importance, that various creeds must be brought back to those portions which they hold in common, and formulas and prayers be drawn up which may suit all alike: thence the desire to transform the great principles and facts of Christianity into symbols left to the interpretations of philosophy; those strange efforts also to unite the revolutionary with the religious spirit; or, lastly, those attempts to deny, or at least consign to oblivion the past of the Catholic church, her traditions, her customs, which ages and events have united with her, and substitute, under the name of Primitive, a newly invented Catholicism. False conceptions, vain endeavours, from which pious feeling and a certain knowledge of our social state have not always been free, but which denote little knowledge of human nature or religion, and a superficial appreciation of the means by which great institutions, whether religious or civil, are founded and endure. No doubt but that Catholicism has something, has much to do in order to adapt itself to all that is new in the world, and to take in our social system the place and part suitable to it. But let it be true to itself, let it not deny its origin, its history, its doctrine, its law; let it not stoop to cowardice or hypocrisy. It would lose its dignity which is essential to its strength, it would fail in obtaining the new strength which it needs. Were I not convinced that harmony may be re-established between the old religion and modern society with truth and honor to both, I would not counsel the attempt. God does not admit of the possibility of falsehood in such high positions for such great objects.

Let, then, *l'Université Catholique* proceed in its course of exact and scrupulous orthodoxy. It is said, I hope truly, that she has many of the clergy for readers. They should be on their guard against attacks on these points. Sometimes, despite appearances of moderation, the attempts succeed, and strike a blow on the vital conditions of their existence. By others they are drawn into the very passions and pursuits from which their mission is mainly intended to keep mankind. Generally such have hitherto had but little success. The most recent example, that of M. l'Abbé de Lamennais, has eventuated in one of the most melancholy spectacles of error and fall that man can present. Surely there are here just reasons for distrust and hesitation. The authors of *l'Université Catholique* are clearly aware of it themselves; for they have been careful to keep themselves clear of these unhappy flights, and to remain, in their own words, "immovably attached to the rock of the Church." They doubtless are so from conviction and duty. They should also be so from prudence, and attend to all the sentiments, scruples, and susceptibilities of the Catholic portion of the public. It is this public especially whom they address, it is the public whom they wish to enlighten, satisfy, reassure, and reconcile with the true progress, the accomplished facts and necessities of our time. That is really the great service wanted by modern society. Let them never lose sight of this essential end. And as to that part of the public which is ruled by the spirit of the age, no doubt their language should reassure and quiet it also, and draw it back to religion, for it has very justly its own susceptibilities and distrusts. But let not the authors of **l'Université Catholique** deceive themselves; they will inspire the public with the greater respect and confidence according as they are themselves found serious and faithful. The public will be the more easily attracted to religion, as she presents herself stable and lofty; for, in the uneasiness which is now prevalent, the public aspire to something fixed and elevated, despite of the passions which still keep it wavering and abased.

Whilst in Catholicism this new religious and social movement, of which **l'Université Catholique** appears to be the most serious manifestation, is beginning, an analogous work is going on in the other Christian communions, and reveals itself by remarkable signs. For many years something fruitful and active has been at work in French Protestantism. Almost immediately after the establishment of peace and international relations in 1814, the English dissenters, struck by the languid state of religion in France, and animated by faith and a strong desire for proselytism, undertook the task of awaking amidst their continental co-religionists the religious spirit, or, more precisely, Protestant Christian feelings. Journeys, correspondence, publications, sermons, pious associations—of which some, as the Bible Society, the Society for the Propagation of the Gospel, the Religious Tract Society, possess extent and notoriety—were the instruments used to forward their design; a design which excited and still excites in French Protestantism some trouble and embarrassment. The established Protestant church was moved. Indifference took offence. Toleration and reason felt some alarm. Impressions not altogether at first void of reason; facts which deserve observation and watchfulness, but of which the importance in our society, and with the guarantees of our laws and customs, is, in my opinion, much less than that of the religious feeling which roused them, and its character and results. The Christian faith, the real and profound faith in the constituent dogmas of Christianity, is springing up again amidst Protestants, but accompanied by that liberty and assiduous search which alter the form of unity but keep up religious vitality; which cares less for the government of men's minds than for the internal life of their souls. This life has its instincts, its imperious and everlasting wants. There is no indifference, no authority, which does or can abolish or cause to be long forgotten the essential and eternal problems of our nature and destiny. Whence does evil spring in the world and in ourselves? How is it to be escaped? Is our own liberty sufficient? Is God's power over and in us needed? What are the relations here below and hereafter between God and our souls? What lot awaits us beyond this life, and how far do our resolutions and actions influence it? This is the definite and practical object of religion. These the questions to which mankind has, through all ages, in all the earth, in every condition, in the confusion of controversy, in the secret heart desired and asked an answer. This is promised to him by Christianity. The dogmas of that faith are replies to these questions, so vital to man generally and individually. These replies are contained in Christian books, and are succeeded by the precepts, the consolation, and the hopes which flow from them. To seek them there, to read them, to draw continually from that spring the means of opposing the evil inclinations, the passions, the weaknesses, the disquiet, the langour of the soul, thereby sustaining it in this world and regenerating it for eternity; such is the Christian Protestant spirit, the spirit which is again animating the French Protestants; the spirit which has had and may again have its faults, like all great ambitions and all great aspirations of the human soul, but which is nevertheless a spirit of true piety and true morality; which suffices for our most exalted intellects, and exercises for all, in all, the most salutary influence over our inward dispositions and outward actions.

Many periodical works, amongst them the **Semeur**, [Footnote 3] and the **Archives of Christianity in the XIX. Century**, are devoted to this spirit, and seek to satisfy and spread it.

[Footnote 3: The **Semeur** has ceased to appear.]

In them all publications, all the incidents which belong at home or abroad to Christian life, are examined, commented on, debated with a reality and earnestness of conviction always rare, but now especially so. Men of rare ability, too, and first of all M. Vinet, professor of French literature at Lausanne, write for the *Semeur*, and often with the most distinguished talent. I might find in these works, even without going very deeply into the question of their doctrines, some traces of political radicalism, very injurious to religion; and also, in matters of religion, traces of a severe and somewhat exclusive spirit, which, when dominant, tends to sectarianism and fanaticism. But clearly here as elsewhere the good spirit of the age, the spirit of light, of justice, and universal benevolence will every day make its way; will clothe the religious spirit of ideas and sentiments in words which will suit them admirably, but which they have not always worn. And thus here as elsewhere I prefer dwelling on what is good to what is evil. When the movement which is good preponderates, I believe in its power; I trust to it, strenuous as may be the opposition, tardy as its progress may appear.

Have we not besides, in liberty, liberty of conscience and speech, the most certain and efficacious of guarantees against fanaticism and religious despotism. **L'Université Catholique** maintains, and will unceasingly uphold the maxims, traditions, and laws of Catholicism. At her side, the spirit of Protestantism reveals herself full of faith and vigour. And as in the bosom of Protestantism the **Semeur** and the **Archives of Christianity** do not express the feelings of all, other collections—the **Protestant Review**, the **Free Enquiry**, the **Evangelist**—labour to make clear and nourish another idea, more scientific, more attached to modern notions and a national church, more occupied in enlightening than deeply stirring the mind.

I do not doubt but that, in this fresh springing up of different beliefs, men interested in their success, and the different sections of the public whom they address, reciprocally inspire but little mistrust or disquiet; that the remembrance of ancient dislikes, ancient animosity still lurk in many a heart, and may break out afresh. It may be occasionally discerned, with all its want of reflection and its harshness. However, take it altogether, the spirit of antipathy and contest, which has so long prevailed in the religious sphere, is becoming weaker and less common. Each creed is more occupied about itself than about others; more anxious to impress the hearts that are inclined to its reception or have received it, than quarrel with those who maintain their own belief. This is the natural result of liberty, and the check imposed on every belief by the civil power which sustains it. It is also the most favourable condition for the very creeds themselves, as obliging them to proceed directly towards their true object, and prevents them from turning aside to alter or lower themselves in despotism or rebellion.

The spirit of religion comes again into the world to conquer but not to usurp. Religious creeds rise and increase together, at once free and contented; free to elevate themselves, to elevate souls to heaven, restrained by their mental liberty and by the independence of the civil power. Let us honor the community in the bosom of which such a sight is possible! It needs, it absolutely needs that religion should step in to purify and strengthen it; but religion can do her work there without dishonor or sacrifice, and when she can, it becomes her bounden duty to do so.

Catholicism, Protestantism, And Philosophy In France.

(*July*, 1838.)

It is of Catholicism and Protestantism, not of religion or even Christianity in general, that I wish to speak.

I regret that I cannot find a word to suit me better than **Philosophy**. The nature of things forbids it. But in order to make myself at once and clearly understood, I hasten to say that I here call **Philosophy** every opinion which disclaims, under whatever name or shape, any faith as restrictive of human thought, and which leaves thought, in religious matters as in all others, free to believe or not to believe, and guide itself by its own authority.

It is also of France, and France alone, that I speak. The condition of Catholicism, Protestantism, and Philosophy is not the same in France and elsewhere, after our moral and social revolutions, as it is in countries which have not undergone such changes. I wish to say nothing but that which results from and applies to precise facts. The time has arrived in such matters for dealing with real facts, and setting aside general terms which avoid the questions they affect to settle.

I am convinced that Catholicism, Protestantism, and Philosophy, in the bosom of the novel state of society in France under the Charter, can live peaceably, both as regards themselves and society; in peace not only material but moral, not only obligatory but voluntary,—without submission, without abasement,—both with truth and with honor.

I wish to prove it.

I repeat my first position. This peace must be established; it is necessary.

Look at the state of things.

Catholicism, Protestantism, Philosophy, and modern French society can neither destroy one another, nor change nor remodel themselves as they wish.

They are facts, old, powerful, living, and indestructible from the remotest times. They have resisted the longest and most severe trials, ages of order and days of chaos.

For ages has new France, the France of the Charter, been forming itself and increasing. Every thing has opposed it, yet everything has contributed to its triumph, the church, nobility, royalty, the court, the greatness of Louis XIV., the inactivity of Louis XV., the wars of the empire, the peace after the restoration. She has surmounted even her own faults, as well as the efforts of her enemies.

Catholicism was born at the same time and in the same cradle as modern Europe. It has associated itself with all the labours of European civilization. It has survived all its transformations. In our own days it has sustained the most terrible shock that has ever been encountered by a creed and a church. It has been raised up again by the hands of the very destroyers themselves. It appears again. Enter the family circle, traverse the country, then will be seen what the power of Catholicism is, in spite of the lukewarmness of many of the faithful members—even of many of the priests.

The lot of Protestantism in France has been hard. It has had against it the king and the people, the literati of the seventeenth, the philosophers of the eighteenth century; at one time it appeared as if extirpated by Catholicism, at another as absorbed by philosophy. It has yielded neither to persecution nor ridicule. It still exists, and is no sooner restored to liberty than it exhibits all its ancient fervour.

As for Philosophy, she has sustained many checks amidst her triumphs. It is easy to set forth her follies and mistakes. She has much to amend in what is past, but nothing to fear for the future. Most of the principles which she proclaimed have become rights. The rights have become facts. The new social condition to which philosophy has given rise will not be more averse to her than the old one which she has overcome.

These are all clearly powers full of life, and which a long futurity awaits. They have struggled roughly but in vain. They have been unable to destroy each other.

They will neither change or perish. No doubt they will modify themselves according to their new position. They will listen to reason. They will bow to necessity, but without renouncing their principles or sacrificing their nature. They can make no such concession. What characteristics and vitality they have must remain. To renounce this would be to die.

Thus, without metamorphosis and as God and time have made them, are these powers called to dwell side by side under the same social roof.

What will happen if they do not live in peace, sincere peace?

Shall we again see the old wars which our fathers have seen?

War between Catholicism and Protestantism? Between religious creeds and philosophy? Between the Church and the new-modelled State? Shall we see a revival of every fanaticism, lay and clerical, philosophic and religious?

It is not likely. Here and there, indeed, in books, in newspapers, even in the gravest publications, hints are given of such a restoration of things: attacks by Catholics on Protestant impiety, by Protestants against popish idolatry, by devotees against reason and its lights, by philosophers against faith and the clergy. A war of words, often sincere, frequently cold, always powerless. Doubtless, the old leaven of hatred and war, deep laid in every human heart, still exists, but it will no more arouse society. Customs as well as laws will prevent this. Even the inclination will soon fail those most anxious for it. The voices which still preach this strife, passionate, radical, and mortal, either of Christian communities between themselves, or of Philosophy against Christianity, are the voices of dying men, already deserted on the battle-field where they persist in staying. This is rather what will happen.

Living neither in peace nor at war, forced to admit vicinity without friendship, and distrust without violence, Catholicism, Protestantism, Philosophy, and in their train society in general, will descend, grow cold, and languish. The dignity and power which spring from truly moral communications will be equally wanting in all. A dry and barren spirit will prevail in relations which are purely official and matters of routine; and we should see spreading and strengthening itself, becoming permanent and in some sort legally consecrated, that spirit of indifference at the same time disdainful yet subordinate, cold yet insecure. This is the lot of societies which are kept together by the bond of administrative regulations alone, void of moral life, that is, of faith and devotion.

Was it then to arrive at this state of things, that for ages human genius displayed itself so gloriously in our country? Was it to end at last in this degradation that all the great creeds, all the moral forces, have contended with so much eagerness and glory for the empire of our society?

They must save it and themselves from this disgraceful peril. They must accept, respect, and loyally serve the new social state; they must learn to live amicably together in its bosom.

I say **they must!** It is an immense point in a great work to look upon success as indispensable and vital. The feeling of necessity gives to those whom that necessity pleases, much power; to the opposite party much resignation. A passionate desire supports even more than it deceives. And here there is indeed room for such a desire; for, during a long future, the honor and moral repose of society are at stake. It cannot remain in this state of apathy and uneasiness in which the mind languishes and exhausts itself. Man desires for his soul more activity and more security, a firmer ground, a higher flight. The true agreement of the great intellectual powers can alone grant him these.

How can this be accomplished?

I grapple at once with the more notorious and serious of the difficulties,—the nature of Catholicism and the conditions of its agreement with the new state of society which has attacked it, and been in its turn so roughly attacked.

I set aside, too, without hesitation, the questions of religion, properly so called; questions which concern the dealings of God with man, questions about the safety of the human soul.

Not that I look on them with indifference, or that their importance is not now as it has always been, overwhelming and immense. It ought, on the contrary, to be frequently repeated, for in our day it has been too much forgotten, and it is the real object, and substance, nay, the essence of religion. The moral quality, the rule of conduct for man in his relations with man, is important. The mental calm and resignation of men in the trials of life is important. The Christian religion teaches these, and thence its great position upon earth and in society. But it does more, it goes far beyond human society and this world. It binds man to God, it reveals to him the secret of this awful tie, it teaches him what he ought to believe and do in respect to his relation to God and his prospect of eternity. Imperishable things from which man may turn aside his gaze, but which do not disappear from his nature; sublime wants from which he cannot free himself, though he may mistake and deny them—the law of these things, the satisfying of these wants, that is to say, the dogma and its consequences, constitute the Christian religion, the first which has really understood and embraced its object.

But in these questions and in the dogmas which reply to them, nothing can now arouse between Catholicism and civil society either conflict or embarrassment. In this matter, the State proclaims not only the liberty but the right of the church, and declares itself absolutely incompetent to interfere. And here lies whatever truth exists in that deplorable and confused saying which has excited so much comment, "***The law is atheistical.***" Surely not so. The law is not atheistical. How should it be so? Is the law a real living being, a being with a soul which approaches to or recedes from God, which may be lost or saved? "Human societies," says M. Royer Collard, "live and die on the earth, there they fulfil their destinies." But they do not comprehend man as an entire. After he has bound himself to society there still remains to him the noblest part of himself, the high faculties by which he raises himself to God, to a future life, to unknown good in an invisible world. We, as individuals, as beings endowed with immortality, have a different destiny from states.

And it is on this account that the State should not interfere with that other destiny. As its nature and aim are different from her own, as the two have nothing in common, to interfere must produce confusion and usurpation.

That which the state now proclaims was taught to it by the Church, the Catholic Church. During centuries when the state wished to interfere in matters of opinion and salvation, did not the Church distinctly reject such pretensions. And how did she do so? By the distinction of temporal and spiritual, of terrestrial and eternal life, that is, by the incompetence of the state to deal with the relations of the soul with God.

And the Catholic Church was right in sustaining this principle, the forgetfulness of which has cost her much. How did she lose a portion of her empire? How came Henry VIII. amongst others to separate from her? By proclaiming the temporal power competent to matters of faith and salvation. Let Catholicism go back to the sixteenth century, to the history of the reformation. It is by the confusion of the two powers, by this religious competence of the state, that she has suffered the rudest shocks. The Catholic Church has no more dangerous enemies than lay theologians, whether princes or doctors.

They are the more dangerous foes because religious motives are not those which alone may animate them, and lay usurpations in matters of faith have often served as a veil to the most worldly interests. Had the religious incompetence of the state always been acknowledged, the church would not so often have seen her property as well as her power in danger or lost.

She has henceforth nothing similar to fear. Usurpation is on both sides forbidden. Her kingdom belongs to herself alone; she possesses it completely and securely.

On this side, the great side of Christian religion in this world, peace is easy and may be sincere between Catholicism and the new social state.

Let us see where the real difficulty exists.

The government of the Catholic Church is a power invested in her own domain, and in matters of faith and salvation, with the character of infallibility.

I put aside, great as they are, all secondary questions, such as the knowledge of the conditions and limits in which infallibility exists, to whom it belongs, to the Holy Seat or to Councils, or to the Holy Seat and Councils united. I look to the one principle which is found in every combination and form of Catholic belief.

The principle itself is founded on the perpetuity of divine revelation, faithfully preserved in the church by means of tradition, and renewed when needful by the inspiration of the Holy Spirit, which ceases not to descend on the successor of St. Peter who was placed at the head of the church by Jesus Christ himself.

This is the essential and vital principle, the base and summit, the Alpha and Omega of Catholicism.

Against a power of such a nature and origin, where it really manifests itself, all discussion, resistance, and separation are unlawful.

The new state of society and constitutional France has its principle also, which has become that of its government.

All human power is fallible, and must be controlled and limited.

Every human society has the right of controlling and limiting, directly and indirectly, in such and such measures, and under such or such form, the power which it obeys.

I do not soften the problem. I set forth the two principles. They are essentially different; they are said to be hostile.

They would be so indeed, could they meet and display themselves in the same sphere. But here I find the remedy I sought.

When ages ago the church so loudly and vehemently insisted on the distinction of the spiritual and temporal, she was acting in the interest of her own dignity and founding her own liberty. She was doing more. She thereby maintained the dignity of man, and laid the foundations of liberty of conscience.

The separation of spiritual from temporal, the doctrine of the church; and the separation of the religious and civil state, the doctrine of our constitutional regime; the independence of religious society in matters of faith, conquered by the church in the earlier days of modern Europe; and liberty of conscience, a victory achieved by modern society,—have one and the same principle at the root. The application and form may be different, the origin and moral signification entirely agree.

Hence the means of peace and harmony between Catholicism and our new society.

Suppose that the two principles, the separation of spiritual and temporal, of the religious and civil state, were (and it is possible, since at the root they agree) sincerely and completely allowed, respected and practised by church and state; whence would the conflict spring?

The Catholic church would loudly maintain her infallibility in the religious sphere, that is, as regards the connexion between spiritual power and the faithful. The state would insist upon liberty of conscience and thought in the social sphere, that is, in the relations of the temporal power with the citizens. Each power would advance according to its principles, parallel, and without collision.

What then is the obstacle?

It is rather historical than reasonable. It arises from the passed deeds and ancient life of the two powers, rather than from their essential principles and actual relations.

The separation of the spiritual and temporal originates in the chaos of the middle ages. It sprung from thence, as the sun appears through a dark and stormy sky. Principles and powers, ideas and situations, all have been in our Europe wonderfully obscure, confused, incoherent, incomplete. There has long been a depth of temporal affairs mixed with spiritual, spiritual with temporal, in the existence and constitution of the church and state. Hence the temptations and attempts, both frequent and terrible, at reciprocal usurpation. The confusion of facts and violence of passions struggled incessantly against the principle which strove to restrain them.

That is the lot of truth here. It is boasted of but disdained, invoked yet rejected, at once admitted and proscribed; here supreme, there powerless. Man deserves no better, the world fares no better than that.

However, after many efforts on certain memorable days some truth does detach itself, and rises so high that she shines brightly and commands respect.

The separation of the spiritual and temporal has had this fortune. Church and state, bishops and philosophers, opinion and law have contributed in turn to secure it for her. It is a principle now so well established amongst us, that neither persons nor things, neither mind nor art, could be kept long clear from its influence.

Since the great ambitions which have disturbed the world be but foolish pretensions, it behoves them carefully to avoid the last risk they can run, that of becoming ridiculous squabbles. Let the two powers, instead of painfully lowering themselves to seize though but for a few days, some fragments from the past confusion, admit fully both as regards right and deed their mutual incompetence; let each establish itself firmly in its special sphere, let each loudly proclaim its principle—the Catholic church, its infallibility in religious orders; the State, the liberty of thought in social concerns. Not only will they then live in peace, but they will respect and serve themselves really in spirit and in truth, and not in a superficial appearance which is unworthy of both.

I say they will respect each other in spirit and in truth, and I regret that I can but glance at the subject. Certainly, setting aside all faith and law, the vital principle of Catholicism, the religious infallibility of the church,—and the vital principle of our civil society, the liberty of conscience and thought,—have a right to the respect, the former of the boldest thinkers, the latter of the most pious and the strictest minds. But I have not room here to enter suitably on such a question; I may attempt it some day.

As to the practical benefits of a true pacification to the Catholic Church and to constitutional France, they are immense. What is the prevailing ill of our temporal society?

The weakening of authority. I do not allude to that strength which insists on being obeyed. Never had power greater command of it; never perhaps so much. I allude to that authority recognized beforehand on principle in a general way, received and felt as a right which is not obliged to resort to force; that authority before which the spirit bows without abasement of heart, and which speaks from on high with the influence not of constraint, but nevertheless of necessity.

That is truly authority. It is not the only principle of the social state. It does not suffice for the government of men. But without it nothing will suffice; neither argument unceasingly persevered in, nor well-understood interest, nor the material preponderance of numbers. Where authority is wanting, whatever the force, obedience is precarious or mean, even near the extreme of rebellion or of servility. Catholicism has the essence of authority; it is authority itself, systematically conceived and organised. It lays it down in principle, and puts it in practice with great firmness of teaching, and a rare intelligence of human nature.

Did this spirit prevail in our society, or did it lean towards it, there would be need to seek elsewhere counterbalances and limits. But the danger is clearly not there; and whilst our institutions and manners cherish in us the spirit of individual independence in thought as well as life, it is a great blessing to society, to its morality as well as its repose, that other causes, other methods of teaching maintain the principle of authority and the spirit of internal submission.

"I learnt in the army what one learns no where else—respect;" said an old retired non-commissioned officer of the Imperial Guard, in 1820.

Catholicism is the greatest, the most holy school of respect that the world has ever seen. France was brought up in this school, in spite of the ill use which human passions have often made of her precepts. The abuse is now little formidable; the benefit ought to be great, for we have great need of it.

Catholicism itself is suffering at present from a grievous malady.

This is the prevailing coldness and routine, the predominance of form over foundation, of external practice over internal feelings.

This arises from the often hypocritical incredulity of the eighteenth century, not very distant from the nineteenth; and also from the preponderance, which has long been excessive, in the church, of the government over the vital principle, of ecclesiastical authority over religious life.

Some analogy existed in this respect between the church and state in the last century. On both sides power was afoot with its old organization, in the hands of its former possessors; but amongst the subjects there was little faith and little love.

What is it, nevertheless, that has saved Catholicism from shipwreck? It is that it was a popular religion and faith. The Catholic government yielded, the Catholic people survived. M. de Monlosier was right; in our days, too, it was the cross of wood which saved the world.

The safety is yet incomplete. The church has risen, but many a soul languishes. Catholicism needs faith, a more inward and lively faith.

It is the vague and ill-regulated feeling of this want, which has for some time inspired those dreams of absolute independence, of rupture between church and state, those shiverings of the fever of democracy, which, under the name of M. l'Abbé de Lamennais, have scandalised the faithful and made the indifferent smile.

Mad, shameful dreams which urge Catholicism to abjure her principles and history, to hand herself over to the contagion of modern evil and to dishonour while she destroys herself.

It is not in such devious ways that Catholicism will find religious life. This will, on the contrary, be found by her remaining faithful to herself in the new position frankly accepted. This position is worthy, strong, favorable to the progress of faith and fervour. It possesses towards the state a fair measure of liberty and alliance, towards the faithful the suitable independence as well as the needful intimacy; no evil hopes, no worldly distractions, nothing which can render zeal impure or even suspected; but nothing, on the other hand, which attacks the traditions or customs of the Church, nothing which tends to deprive it of the august character of elevation and stability. The Catholic Church is thus placed in constitutional France; and success, religious and social, belong to the use of proper measures, as by proper measures success is certain.

The situation of Protestantism is more simple: some persons even affect to consider it more favourable. The general feeling which prevails in our days, our political and domestic alliances, the analogy of principle between constitutional France and Protestant England, all seem to say that Protestantism is in favour. There are some even who pretend to the discovery of a plot to make France Protestant.

This does not deserve even a passing remark.

There was a time, not very distant, when Protestantism did not seem so well placed in France. I do not speak of the Restoration; even under the empire it was often said that Protestantism had a republican tendency, that her maxims were contrary to stability and power. The spirits of Protestantism and revolution were considered as related.

This is still repeated. It has become a party theme; and Protestantism is perseveringly represented as incompatible with social order, peaceful dispositions, and monarchy.

Happily, Protestantism is not a thing of yesterday in Europe; it appeals to history and facts for a reply.

If there be any where three countries which, for fifty years, amidst the overthrow of ideas, states, and dynasties have given striking proofs of affection for their institutions and princes, for the conservative and monarchical spirit, they are assuredly England, Holland, Prussia—three Protestant countries, *the* three Protestant countries *par excellence* in Europe; countries, too, wonderful for order, for industry, and for prosperity; countries which greatly conduce to the power and glory of modern civilization. There can be no more decisive answer to the worn out declamations of ancient party spirit, nor do they deserve more ample discussion.

French Protestantism is peculiarly free from this ridiculous reproach. It has not been remarkable for receiving too much protection or justice. It enjoys them as a new acquisition, with modesty and gratitude. Never was a religious society disposed to evince towards the civil power greater deference and respect.

Protestantism, by a singular amalgamation, has been blamed for too much deference even in this respect. It has been accused of lowering religion, and making the church subservient to the state. This, it is said, is the consequence of the fall of the ecclesiastical hierarchy, the great governing power of the Catholic church, which Protestantism has attacked. Thus the division between spiritual and temporal has disappeared; the spiritual has fallen under the yoke of the civil power.

I have already said sufficient of the separation of spiritual and temporal, to avoid the suspicion of thinking ill of it. It is one of the most glorious forms which, in modern Europe, the independence of thought and faith has assumed. It is the principle in virtue of which Catholicism must, in the midst of modern institutions and ideas, assume a worthy and secure place.

But in spiritual as in temporal order, it is necessary that liberty have but one aspect and be exclusively attached to this or that combination. Religion has more than one method of preserving her dignity and independence; God plants it and causes it to prosper in more than one soil, in more than one climate.

In fact, taking things together, faith has been strong, and conscience has displayed itself with energy in Protestant countries, in spite of the doubtful lines of demarcation between the two domains, and the too frequent intervention of the civil power in religious matters.

This is because the civil power has never made religious matters its chief concern. Politics, governments, properly so called, have absorbed its attention and power. Sooner or later, it has ended by leaving consciences to themselves; it has, at all events, left the reins more loose and the field more free than has been the case in Catholic countries, where there has been a power devoted to the sole task of ruling spiritual society.

Thus, too, there is in every society, political or religious, a certain intimate and permanent tendency which gets the better of all forms of organization and all accidents of situation. Protestantism sprang from free enquiry. It is her standard. It has never been abandoned by her, whatever share she may have taken in the civil rule; I will go so far as to say, the civil despotism. In short, human thought, in religion as in every other matter, has displayed itself with infinite activity and freedom in Protestant countries.

Do we forget, besides, the first and most powerful cause of spiritual independence? It is that Protestantism,—she cannot avoid it,—admits into her bosom great differences of faith and practice, dissents, separations, sects in short. She may have often condemned and persecuted them, but she has never deemed herself obliged to curse and extirpate them. They have lived and multiplied under Protestantism, in the teeth of the national church; ill-treated, humiliated, but never forced from some last retreat; always, to a certain degree, protected by the spirit of free enquiry, its examples and recollections. This affords a strong pledge for liberty of conscience, and opens an asylum to all who may have been attacked or vexed on account of their faith by the civil power. If the Anglican church has, with some justice, though much exaggeration, been accused of complaisance towards the temporal sovereign, the English dissenters have, on the other hand, unceasingly proclaimed their haughty independence of her. The shield which the Catholic church has found in the separation of the spiritual and temporal, has been found by Protestantism in the freedom, even though incomplete, of religious dissent and the multiplicity of sects.

And as a just reward for this dawn of liberty, the Protestant sects are not so widely severed as they appear to be from the national Church and the State. Persecuted, irritated, even rebellious, they have nevertheless strongly adhered, with hidden yet deep feeling, to the common centre of belief and the public destiny. An ardent Puritan was, under Queen Elizabeth, sent to the pillory and condemned to have his hand cut off. The hand falls; with his left, he raises his large hat, crying "God save the Queen!" Almost invariably in critical circumstances, when the vital interests of the national religion or of the country appeared to be compromised, the English dissenters have rallied round the state, and though forsaking her religious banner, have still served her with exemplary devotion.

I have little taste for sectarian spirit, but never should Protestantism when in power set up as a national church, and treat dissenters with rigour or disdain; for it owes in part to them the maintenance of its dignity, as well as the fervour of faith and the progress of liberty of conscience. Above all, never should our constitutional monarchy trouble itself about dissent, should it one day arise, in French Protestantism. It could not possess political importance, or tend to weaken the tie which binds the Protestants of France to the new social condition and its governing power.

Protestantism, while free from political danger, has, in a purely religious point of view, much good to do in France; not by drawing France to her standard, by converting her, to use the customary phrase. Conversions on either side are and will henceforward be few, and the importance which some persons attach to them as a matter of joy or regret is somewhat puerile. It is a step and a most important step for the individuals, but one of no social moment. France will not become Protestant. Protestantism will not become extinct in France. One reason among many is decisive. The struggle of these days of ideas and empire is not between Catholicism and Protestantism. Impiety and immorality are the enemies which both have to resist. To restore the spirit of religion is the work to which both are called. The work, like the evil, is immense. A slight probing of the wound, a short but serious glance at the moral state of the masses of men, whose minds are so fluctuating, whose hearts so empty, who desire so much and hope so little, who pass so rapidly from the excitement of fever to mental torpor,—and the observer will be penetrated with sadness and alarm. Catholics or Protestants, priests or laymen, be ye whom ye may, do not, if believers, be uneasy about each other; reserve that for those who believe not. There is the field for work, there the harvest. The field is open to Protestantism as to Catholicism; work will not be wanting to either; each has the aptitude and peculiar qualities to enable it to labour with success.

We suffer from very different moral complaints.

Some are above all things wearied and disgusted with the uncertainty and disorder of men's minds. They need a harbour sheltered from every point, a light which is ever steady, a guiding hand which never trembles. They ask from religion rather support to weakness than aliment for activity. They require her, while elevating, to sustain them; while touching their hearts, to keep down their understandings; while animating their inward life, to give them at the same time, and above all else, a deep sense of security.

Catholicism is wonderfully adapted to this frame of mind, now so common. She has gratifications for desires, remedies for suffering. She knows how at once to subdue and to please. Her grasp is strong, her prospects full of charm for the imagination. She excels in occupying while soothing the soul, which she suits after periods of great fatigue; for without leaving it cold or idle, she saves it much trouble, and undertakes for it the burden of responsibility.

For another class of minds, though also suffering and separated from religion, more intellectual and physical activity is required. They too feel the need of returning to God and the faith; but they are used to examine everything themselves, and only to receive that which they acquire by their own labour. They wish to shun incredulity, but liberty is dear to them; there is in their religious tendency more thirst than lassitude. To such, Protestantism may gain access, for while it speaks to them of piety and faith, it encourages and invites them to make use of their reason and liberty. It has been accused of coldness. That is a mistake. In ceaselessly appealing to free and personal examination it takes deep root in the soul, and becomes easily an inward faith, in which the activity of the understanding keeps up instead of extinguishing the fervour of the heart. And hence its connexion with the modern spirit, which formerly in its youth was at the same time reasoning and enthusiastic, eager for conviction as for liberty, and which, despite its momentary quiescence, has retained its old nature and will infallibly resume its double character.

Catholicism and Protestantism must never lose sight of our system of society, for it is on this that they must work. Let each of them appeal to it in its own way, looking for and attending to the wounds or wants for the cure or satisfaction of which they are best calculated. That is their true, their efficacious and disinterested mission, not looking at each other and seeking a renewal of controversy.

In general, I believe controversy is but of little use, and has little religious effect. In every age it has taken but a small part in the triumph of great moral truths. They establish themselves, especially at their first appearing, by direct and dogmatic exposition. We have in the gospels the most remarkable and august example. From their earliest day, neither motive or occasion of controversy was wanting with Jew or pagan. Yet we scarcely meet with it in the preaching either of Jesus Christ or of the apostles. They lay down their rule of faith, their precepts; they knock without ceasing at the doors of the hearts which they desire to enter. They do not trouble themselves to argue with their adversaries. Controversy arises later, and when it does, it soon disfigures the truth, for it distributes it in fragments among parties, sects, men; and each holds fast, with the intractable blindness of self-love, to the fragment which has fallen to his lot, in which he wishes to see, and that others should see, truth in her entirety.

Let them keep clear of controversy; let them attend little to each other, much to themselves and their task. Catholicism and Protestantism will then dwell peaceably, not only within its new state, but together.

I know that this peace will not be that spiritual unity which has been so talked of. Spiritual unity, beautiful in itself, is in this world chimerical; and from chimerical it becomes tyrannical.

As finite and free beings, that is to say, incomplete and fallible, unity escapes us, and we constantly miss it.

Harmony in liberty is the only unity to which men here below can pretend. Or, rather, it is for them the best, the only mode of elevation towards that true unity which all violence, all constraint,—that is, every invasion of spiritual by material order,—throws back and obscures, under the pretext of attaining it.

Harmony in liberty is the spirit of Christianity. It is charity united with zeal. It is also the object of philosophy, for it is the true, the moral sense of the principle of toleration and equal protection of the rites of worship; a principle which impiety has violated by trying to set it up as the standard of indifference and contempt for religion, but which allies itself wondrously with zeal and faith, for on *their* right it is itself founded.

The alliance must be ratified. I say *must* in concluding, as I did when beginning. Peace between religious creeds is now imposed on all alike by our social condition. Harmony in liberty is their legal condition, their charter. Let them yield to it in spirit as in act; let them love it while obeying it. I fear not the fate of a false prophet, when I predict that religion will be thereby as great a gainer as society.

As to Philosophy, she has in our days the glory of not having remained a Utopia. From discoveries she has proceeded to conquests. She has metamorphosed her ideas into facts and institutions; a formidable change, as it reveals not only the errors of the first thought, but for a time misleads and corrupts it by plunging it into the vortex of human passions;

nevertheless a great glory, and one which assigns to philosophy a high position in the new social state.

It is a rare privilege to be able, without embarrassment, worthily to acknowledge and abjure error. Philosophy can do this, for, politically speaking, victory belongs to her, and not only victory but power. Though much self-deceived, she has done much. She has reason for pride as well as for modesty. She can afford to show herself just, benevolent, and respectful to her former adversaries. She cannot be charged with weakness or cowardice.

Practically, experience has enlightened her. She knows better than she did the true condition of morality and human society. She knows that she herself is not all-sufficient, that she suffices not entirely for souls or nations, that in human nature and in the general course of affairs the share due to religion is immense, and that philosophy should not contest it with her.

To go still deeper, philosophy herself is about to become seriously and sincerely religious. Like Catholicism, like Protestantism, she cannot change her nature, she must remain philosophy, that is to say free and independant thought, whatever her field of action. But as regards religious questions, she sees that she has often been short-sighted and hasty, that neither impiety nor indifference constitutes true knowledge, that the proudest spirit may humble itself before God, and that there is philosophy in faith itself.

All this is still very vague, and I speak but vaguely of it. However, so it is. It is on this slope that philosophy is now placed, and along it that she must hereafter advance. Her future must be great in the midst of that society which she has formed. The future must be great for spiritual order as a whole, religious and philosophical. May this destiny be accomplished! May spiritual order recover her activity and renown, with a peace and harmony hitherto unknown. Therein consists the dignity of man! therein the strength of society.